TABLE OF CONTENTS

RECIPE	MEAL TYPE	
#1		
#2		
#3		
#4		
#5		
#6		
#7		
#8		
#9		
#10		
#11		
#12		
#13		
#14		
#15		
#16		
#17		
#18		
#19		
#20		
#21		
#22		
#23		
#24		
#25		
#26		
#27		
#28		
#29		
#30		
#31		
#32		
#33		

TABLE OF CONTENTS

RECIPE	MEAL TYPE	NAME
#34		
#35		
#36		
#37		
#38		
#39		
#40		
#41		
#42		
#43		
#44		
#45		
#46		
#47		
#48		
#49		
#50		
#51		
#52		
#53		
#54		
#55		
#56		
#57		
#58		
#59		
#60		
#61		
#62		
#63		
#64	MEAL TYPE	NAME
#65		
#66		

TABLE OF CONTENTS

RECIPE	MEAL TYPE	NAME
#67		
#68		
#69		
#70		
#71		
#72		
#73		
#74		
#75		
#76		
#77		
#78		
#79		
#80		
#81		
#82		
#83		
#84		
#85		
#86		
#87		
#88		
#89		
#90		
#91		
#92		
#93		
#94		
#95		
#96		
#97		
#98		
#99		

#1

SERVES

PREP TIME   COOK TIME

INGREDIENTS

INSTRUCTIONS

NOTES

SERVES

PREP TIME   COOK TIME

INGREDIENTS

INSTRUCTIONS

NOTES

Recipe #3

SERVES

PREP TIME   COOK TIME

INGREDIENTS

INSTRUCTIONS

NOTES

SERVES

PREP TIME   COOK TIME

INGREDIENTS

INSTRUCTIONS

NOTES

SERVES

PREP TIME   COOK TIME

INGREDIENTS

INSTRUCTIONS

NOTES

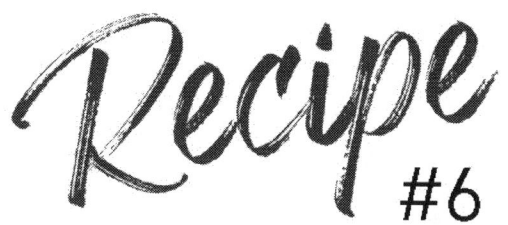

SERVES

PREP TIME   COOK TIME

INGREDIENTS

INSTRUCTIONS

NOTES

#7

SERVES

PREP TIME   COOK TIME

INGREDIENTS

INSTRUCTIONS

NOTES

#8

SERVES

PREP TIME   COOK TIME

INGREDIENTS

INSTRUCTIONS

NOTES

SERVES

PREP TIME   COOK TIME

INGREDIENTS

INSTRUCTIONS

NOTES

SERVES

PREP TIME   COOK TIME

INGREDIENTS

INSTRUCTIONS

NOTES

#11

SERVES
PREP TIME   COOK TIME

INGREDIENTS

INSTRUCTIONS

NOTES

SERVES

PREP TIME   COOK TIME

INGREDIENTS

INSTRUCTIONS

NOTES

#13

SERVES

PREP TIME   COOK TIME

INGREDIENTS

INSTRUCTIONS

NOTES

#14

SERVES

PREP TIME   COOK TIME

INGREDIENTS

INSTRUCTIONS

NOTES

Recipe #15

SERVES

PREP TIME   COOK TIME

INGREDIENTS

INSTRUCTIONS

NOTES

SERVES

PREP TIME   COOK TIME

INGREDIENTS

INSTRUCTIONS

NOTES

SERVES

PREP TIME   COOK TIME

INGREDIENTS

INSTRUCTIONS

NOTES

SERVES

PREP TIME   COOK TIME

INGREDIENTS

INSTRUCTIONS

NOTES

Recipe #19

SERVES

PREP TIME   COOK TIME

INGREDIENTS

INSTRUCTIONS

NOTES

SERVES

PREP TIME   COOK TIME

INGREDIENTS

INSTRUCTIONS

NOTES

SERVES

PREP TIME   COOK TIME

INGREDIENTS

INSTRUCTIONS

NOTES

SERVES

PREP TIME   COOK TIME

INGREDIENTS

INSTRUCTIONS

NOTES

#23

SERVES

PREP TIME   COOK TIME

INGREDIENTS

INSTRUCTIONS

NOTES

#24

SERVES

PREP TIME   COOK TIME

INGREDIENTS

INSTRUCTIONS

NOTES

# #25

SERVES

PREP TIME   COOK TIME

INGREDIENTS

INSTRUCTIONS

NOTES

SERVES

PREP TIME   COOK TIME

INGREDIENTS

INSTRUCTIONS

NOTES

#27

SERVES

PREP TIME   COOK TIME

INGREDIENTS

INSTRUCTIONS

NOTES

SERVES

PREP TIME   COOK TIME

INGREDIENTS

INSTRUCTIONS

NOTES

SERVES

PREP TIME   COOK TIME

INGREDIENTS

INSTRUCTIONS

NOTES

SERVES

PREP TIME   COOK TIME

INGREDIENTS

INSTRUCTIONS

NOTES

Recipe #31

SERVES

PREP TIME   COOK TIME

INGREDIENTS

INSTRUCTIONS

NOTES

SERVES

PREP TIME   COOK TIME

INGREDIENTS

INSTRUCTIONS

NOTES

SERVES

PREP TIME   COOK TIME

INGREDIENTS

INSTRUCTIONS

NOTES

#34

SERVES

PREP TIME   COOK TIME

INGREDIENTS

INSTRUCTIONS

NOTES

SERVES

PREP TIME   COOK TIME

INGREDIENTS

INSTRUCTIONS

NOTES

SERVES

PREP TIME   COOK TIME

INGREDIENTS

INSTRUCTIONS

NOTES

SERVES

PREP TIME   COOK TIME

INGREDIENTS

INSTRUCTIONS

NOTES

SERVES

PREP TIME   COOK TIME

INGREDIENTS

INSTRUCTIONS

NOTES

#39

SERVES

PREP TIME   COOK TIME

INGREDIENTS

INSTRUCTIONS

NOTES

SERVES

PREP TIME   COOK TIME

INGREDIENTS

INSTRUCTIONS

NOTES

Recipe #41

SERVES

PREP TIME   COOK TIME

INGREDIENTS

INSTRUCTIONS

NOTES

SERVES

PREP TIME   COOK TIME

INGREDIENTS

INSTRUCTIONS

NOTES

SERVES

PREP TIME   COOK TIME

INGREDIENTS

INSTRUCTIONS

NOTES

SERVES

PREP TIME   COOK TIME

INGREDIENTS

INSTRUCTIONS

NOTES

#45

SERVES

PREP TIME   COOK TIME

INGREDIENTS

INSTRUCTIONS

NOTES

SERVES

PREP TIME   COOK TIME

INGREDIENTS

INSTRUCTIONS

NOTES

SERVES

PREP TIME   COOK TIME

INGREDIENTS

INSTRUCTIONS

NOTES

SERVES

PREP TIME   COOK TIME

INGREDIENTS

INSTRUCTIONS

NOTES

#49

SERVES

PREP TIME   COOK TIME

INGREDIENTS

INSTRUCTIONS

NOTES

SERVES

PREP TIME   COOK TIME

INGREDIENTS

INSTRUCTIONS

NOTES

SERVES

PREP TIME   COOK TIME

INGREDIENTS

INSTRUCTIONS

NOTES

SERVES

PREP TIME

COOK TIME

INGREDIENTS

INSTRUCTIONS

NOTES

SERVES

PREP TIME   COOK TIME

INGREDIENTS

INSTRUCTIONS

NOTES

Recipe #54

SERVES

PREP TIME   COOK TIME

INGREDIENTS

INSTRUCTIONS

NOTES

SERVES

PREP TIME   COOK TIME

INGREDIENTS

INSTRUCTIONS

NOTES

SERVES

PREP TIME   COOK TIME

INGREDIENTS

INSTRUCTIONS

NOTES

SERVES

PREP TIME　　　COOK TIME

INGREDIENTS

INSTRUCTIONS

NOTES

SERVES

PREP TIME   COOK TIME

INGREDIENTS

INSTRUCTIONS

NOTES

SERVES

PREP TIME   COOK TIME

INGREDIENTS

INSTRUCTIONS

NOTES

SERVES

PREP TIME   COOK TIME

INGREDIENTS

INSTRUCTIONS

NOTES

#61

SERVES

PREP TIME   COOK TIME

INGREDIENTS

INSTRUCTIONS

NOTES

SERVES

PREP TIME   COOK TIME

INGREDIENTS

INSTRUCTIONS

NOTES

Recipe #63

SERVES

PREP TIME   COOK TIME

INGREDIENTS

INSTRUCTIONS

NOTES

SERVES

PREP TIME   COOK TIME

INGREDIENTS

INSTRUCTIONS

NOTES

SERVES

PREP TIME   COOK TIME

INGREDIENTS

INSTRUCTIONS

NOTES

#66

SERVES

PREP TIME   COOK TIME

INGREDIENTS

INSTRUCTIONS

NOTES

#67

SERVES

PREP TIME COOK TIME

INGREDIENTS

INSTRUCTIONS

NOTES

SERVES

PREP TIME   COOK TIME

INGREDIENTS

INSTRUCTIONS

NOTES

#69

SERVES

PREP TIME   COOK TIME

INGREDIENTS

INSTRUCTIONS

NOTES

#70

SERVES

PREP TIME   COOK TIME

INGREDIENTS

INSTRUCTIONS

NOTES

SERVES

PREP TIME **COOK TIME**

INGREDIENTS

INSTRUCTIONS

NOTES

SERVES

PREP TIME   COOK TIME

INGREDIENTS

INSTRUCTIONS

NOTES

Recipe #73

SERVES

PREP TIME   COOK TIME

INGREDIENTS

INSTRUCTIONS

NOTES

SERVES

PREP TIME   COOK TIME

INGREDIENTS

INSTRUCTIONS

NOTES

Recipe #75

SERVES

PREP TIME   COOK TIME

INGREDIENTS

INSTRUCTIONS

NOTES

SERVES

PREP TIME   COOK TIME

INGREDIENTS

INSTRUCTIONS

NOTES

SERVES

PREP TIME   COOK TIME

INGREDIENTS

INSTRUCTIONS

NOTES

SERVES

PREP TIME   COOK TIME

INGREDIENTS

INSTRUCTIONS

NOTES

SERVES

PREP TIME   COOK TIME

INGREDIENTS

INSTRUCTIONS

NOTES

SERVES

PREP TIME   COOK TIME

INGREDIENTS

INSTRUCTIONS

NOTES

#81

SERVES

PREP TIME COOK TIME

INGREDIENTS

INSTRUCTIONS

NOTES

#82

SERVES

PREP TIME   COOK TIME

INGREDIENTS

INSTRUCTIONS

NOTES

#83

SERVES

PREP TIME   COOK TIME

INGREDIENTS

INSTRUCTIONS

NOTES

SERVES

PREP TIME   COOK TIME

INGREDIENTS

INSTRUCTIONS

NOTES

#85

SERVES

PREP TIME   COOK TIME

INGREDIENTS

INSTRUCTIONS

NOTES

SERVES

PREP TIME   COOK TIME

INGREDIENTS

INSTRUCTIONS

NOTES

SERVES

PREP TIME   COOK TIME

INGREDIENTS

INSTRUCTIONS

NOTES

SERVES

PREP TIME   COOK TIME

INGREDIENTS

INSTRUCTIONS

NOTES

#89

SERVES

PREP TIME   COOK TIME

INGREDIENTS

INSTRUCTIONS

NOTES

SERVES

PREP TIME

COOK TIME

INGREDIENTS

INSTRUCTIONS

NOTES

SERVES

PREP TIME   COOK TIME

INGREDIENTS

INSTRUCTIONS

NOTES

SERVES

PREP TIME   COOK TIME

INGREDIENTS

INSTRUCTIONS

NOTES

SERVES

PREP TIME   COOK TIME

INGREDIENTS

INSTRUCTIONS

NOTES

SERVES

PREP TIME   COOK TIME

INGREDIENTS

INSTRUCTIONS

NOTES

SERVES

PREP TIME   COOK TIME

INGREDIENTS

INSTRUCTIONS

NOTES

# 96

SERVES

PREP TIME　　　COOK TIME

INGREDIENTS

INSTRUCTIONS

NOTES

SERVES

PREP TIME   COOK TIME

INGREDIENTS

INSTRUCTIONS

NOTES

SERVES

PREP TIME   COOK TIME

INGREDIENTS

INSTRUCTIONS

NOTES

SERVES

PREP TIME   COOK TIME

INGREDIENTS

INSTRUCTIONS

NOTES

#100

SERVES

PREP TIME   COOK TIME

INGREDIENTS

INSTRUCTIONS

NOTES

Made in United States
Orlando, FL
20 February 2024